It's Me Oh Lord!

Early Morning Devotions

IT'S ME OH LORD

Copyright © 2020 Marilyn E Porter.

All rights reserved. No part of this publication may be reproduced, distributed, or transmitted in any form or by any means, including photocopying, recording, or other electronic or mechanical methods, without the prior written permission of the publisher, except in the case of brief quotations embodied in critical reviews and certain other noncommercial uses permitted by copyright law. For permission requests, write to the publisher, addressed "Attention: Permissions Coordinator," at the email address listed: thescatterbrainedgenius@gmail.com

ISBN 978-1-7338696-6-9

IT'S ME OH LORD

Contents

DAILY BIBLE CONFESSSIONS 6
Psalm 63 (KJV) 8
APOSTLE DR. MARILYN E PORTER 9
PASTOR GENAE KULAH 11
PASTOR CASSANDRA ELLIOTT 15
DR. ONIKA SHIRLEY 17
TIESHA C. FRONTIS 20
DR. ONIKA SHIRLEY 23
MINISTER JANEL THOMPSON 26
PASTOR GENAE KULAH 28
DR. ONIKA SHIRLEY 32
STEVII A. MILLS 35
CHRISTINA WILSON 38
DR. ONIKA SHIRLEY 40
PASTOR DENISE ELBERT 43
PASTOR GENAE KULAH 47
DR. ONIKA SHIRLEY 51
DR. ONIKA SHIRLEY 54
PASTOR DENISE ELBERT 57
DR. ONIKA SHIRLEY 60
ABOUT MARILYN E PORTER 69
ABOUT GENAE KULAH 72
ABOUT DENISE ELBERT 73
ABOUT ONIKA SHIRLEY 74
ABOUT CASSANDRA ELLIOTT 76
ABOUT JANEL THOMPSON 78
ABOUT STEVII MILLS 80
ABOUT TIESHA FRONTIS 81

IT'S ME OH LORD

ABOUT JUANITA E GAYNOR 82
ABOUT CHRISTINA WILSON 84
OTHER TITLES 85

DAILY BIBLE CONFESSSIONS

1. I am a daughter of the king, who walks in victory because of the victory that secured by the death, burial, and resurrection of Jesus. I have authority, and peace is my way of life, because of the power (Holy Spirit), who works in me.

2. I do not have to fear coming to God. He wants to shower me with His mercies, which are new every morning.

3. Prayer is daily communication with God, and He wants to speak to me.

4. My choices today will determine my future.

5. Chastisement from God is love in action.

PASTOR GENAE KULAH

IT'S ME OH LORD

IT'S ME OH LORD

Psalm 63 (KJV)

O God, thou art my God; early will I seek thee: my soul thirsteth for thee, my flesh longeth for thee in a dry and thirsty land, where no water is.

2 To see thy power and thy glory, so as I have seen thee in the sanctuary.

3 Because thy lovingkindness is better than life, my lips shall praise thee.

4 Thus will I bless thee while I live: I will lift up my hands in thy name.

5 My soul shall be satisfied as with marrow and fatness; and my mouth shall praise thee with joyful lips:

6 When I remember thee upon my bed and meditate on thee in the night watches.

7 Because thou hast been my help, therefore in the shadow of thy wings will I rejoice.

8 My soul followeth hard after thee: thy right hand upholdeth me.

9 But those that seek my soul, to destroy it, shall go into the lower parts of the earth.

10 They shall fall by the sword: they shall be a portion for foxes.

11 But the king shall rejoice in God; everyone that sweareth by him shall glory: but the mouth of them that speak lies shall be stopped.

Early Morning with

APOSTLE DR. MARILYN E PORTER

All things were made by him; and without him was not anything made that was made.

John 1:3

In the morning when I rise, I am immediately reminded of the love that was bestowed upon me to live! Before my eyes can even focus on the sun or my ears adjust to the audible sounds of nature, I am reminded of the blood that flowed on Calvary – just for me.

Some say that we should embrace the universe, but Jesus paid it all for me, I dear bow down to a tree, or the moon or the rivers and seas, I shall bow to the one whom created all of these!

So, in the morning when I rise, when I open my eyes, I see the train of His glory and the majesty of His sovereignty and I am free.

Prayer

Father God, in the name of Jesus– YOU Master of all things created; the sun, the moon and the stars, keep in your steadfast way that I might forget that YOU alone are God.

Amen.

IT'S ME OH LORD

Early Morning with

PASTOR GENAE KULAH

**Together with Christ Jesus He also raised us up and seated us in the heavens.
Ephesians 2:8**

As women of God we must have a firm understanding regarding our position in life. Often, we get into a situation that we did not intend to be in and begin to act in a way that is contrary to who we are. We do this because we forget who we are and whose we are. I am here today to remind you as well as myself that whatever situation we find our self in, it is not the determining factor for who we are. Even the words people say do not define us unless we allow it. But on the flip side, the words we say do define us, and if they do not line up with what God says about us then we are lying to ourselves.

The word of God says that together, not me but we, with Jesus Christ have been raised up to sit up. When we get a full understanding of why we are raised up to sit up, we will act in a way that shows who we are and whose we are.

We are raised up to sit up to:

- **Have authority over the enemy.** Look, I have given you the authority to trample on snakes and scorpions and over all the power of the enemy; nothing will ever harm you. Luke 10:19
- **Have peace in the middle of chaos.** May the Lord of peace Himself give you peace always in every

way. The Lord be with all of you 2 Thessalonians 3:16

- **Have power to be a witness of God.** But you will receive power when the Holy Spirit has come on you, and you will be My witnesses in Jerusalem, in all Judea and Samaria, and to the ends of the earth." Acts 1:8

This is a clarion call for the women of God to rise up and sit up. No more bowed down heads or broken hearts. As we rise up and sit up, we will draw people to us because there will be something different about us. The difference is the God in us. The one who died, was buried, and rose with all power in His hands and lives in us in the person of the Holy Spirit. Let's take our position today and be about our Father's business.

Prayer

Dear Lord,

Help me to remember that I am an overcomer who has been raised up to sit up. You have given me everything I need to walk according to your purpose. I am your kingdom woman. To you be all the glory.

Amen.

IT'S ME OH LORD

Early Morning with

PASTOR CASSANDRA ELLIOTT

I will never forget. In the early days when I was diagnosed with kidney failure, that I picked up the Bible and read this scripture.

Psalm 28:7 reads –

"The Lord is my strength and my shield; my heart trusted in him and I am helped; therefore, my heart greatly rejoiceth; and with my song, I will praise him."

This scripture reminded me, that God is my strength! The confidence of this caused me to sing! If I trust in Him, he would be my help! I decided to always keep a song in my heart. Even on the day when I finally received a kidney transplant. Before I went into surgery, I decided to sing my song! Even on the operating table I decided to sing. Why? Because God had been my strength, my shield, and my help. I want to encourage you, Keep a song in your heart. Your song will bring comfort and remind you that God will be your strength and shield and help in times of need! You may not sing this song outwardly but internally. And it is something that no one can ever take from you.

Keep Singing!

Prayer

Father God in the name of your Son, Jesus – never take away my voice to sing praises unto You.

Amen.

Early Morning with

DR. ONIKA SHIRLEY

The Lord will keep you from all evil

He will keep your life.

The Lord will keep your going out and your coming in from this time forth and forevermore.

Psalm 121:7-8

The Lord has been my keeper in so many ways. He has kept me all the days of my life. He kept me when things around me could've caused me harm knowingly and unknowingly. He has kept me from all hurt, harm, and danger. He's kept me emotionally stable when the weight of the world rested heavily on my shoulders to a point that I could have lost my mind, and I could have lost my balance. I can't track of how many times His mercy and protection kept me from physical harm, some of which I could have avoided by way of making better decisions. I know that through it all God was right there. He kept me by never leaving me. God never left my side and He never allowed anything to take me all the way. I can honestly say the Lord has been and continues to be my keeper. He has promised to be with me wherever I go

Prayer

Lord Jesus, we live in a fallen world that is troubled with very real challenges. Lord your people are suffering physically, emotionally, and spiritually. Thank you, God, that as the creator of heaven and earth, nothing is beyond your control. Lord, we know that there is no thing that you can't confront and force that you can't bring into submission if it be thy will As we look to you, our very present help, grant us your peace that surpasses all understanding. Lord continue to look down on us and help us see that your hand is still working on our behalf. These blessings we ask in the mighty name of Jesus.

Amen.

IT'S ME OH LORD

Early Morning with

TIESHA C. FRONTIS

"Lord, there are times when I don't feel worthy of coming to you with my problems but right now God, I am Standing in the Need of Prayer. God it is me, please give me the words to say. God give me the strength to form the words. God give me the understanding of every turmoil I am facing right now. I need to hear from you on this very day and time and I will not let go God until you bless me. I may not know every word in the bible, but it is my desire to know you in a more intimate way. Lord, take total control of every situation. I truly yield my will to your will, Oh Lord. So, God please hear my heart."

If you ever find yourself feeling totally worthless, hopeless, discouraged, worn out and in total despair, I encourage you to go to God and just be you. Tell him, "I Give You Me Oh Lord". Be so transparent you have nothing left. You empty out so he can begin to fill you with his love. He is right there to hear your every word those spoken and unspoken.

Prayer

Lord, I pray right now for every person that read these words that you speak to their Spirit and engulf them with your love, peace, strength and understanding so that they can begin to see clearly the path you have for them. I pray that they see themselves as you see them Lord. I pray for their minds and hearts. Re-construct them in a way that every pain they feel is turned around for their good. In Jesus Name Amen.

My Encouragement: God loves you just the way you are. He knows every hair on your head and wants to love you unconditionally. Allow him into your heart. You will feel a weight lifted. You are beautiful. You are loved. You are an overcomer and you are being healed with every tear you cry. Don't lose your Faith. Allow yourself to go through the process and I promise you will come out stronger every time. Love who you are and where you are. Your self-worth matters and remember you will win in the end.

Amen.

Early Morning with

DR. ONIKA SHIRLEY

By grace you have been saved through faith. And this is not your own doing; it is the gift of God.

Ephesians 2:8

Grace is just unmerited favor. There is absolutely nothing that you and I could have done to invoke, to work toward, to influence, to take action on, to achieve the grace that was so graciously given to us by our Lord and Savior Jesus Christ. It was not possible to be done by mere human hands. The grace of God required the divine Son of God Himself, Jesus. He was truly the only one that could have done what was done for you and me. Our Lord and Savior He came but He didn't just come, but He came with a purpose. Jesus came and conquered sin and death. We are graciously given grace by God. God begins His loving relationship with humanity in grace, and He is going to continue in grace with us. It is grace and grace alone that saves, and this must be believed by faith. It is not based on our works or how good we behave, but all the awareness of merit was eliminated at the foot of the cross.

PRAYER

Gracious and Eternal Father thank you for your amazing grace. My God your grace is amazing it saved someone sinking in sin like me. Father I was wretched and drowning in my sin and I know I don't deserve your unmerited favor, but God you gave me the gift in spite of me. You paid a ransom for me with your Son Jesus's life. Father God thank you for giving us a gift that we could never deserve. Thank you, Father, that we don't have to earn an ounce of the plentiful grace that flows freely for us every day. Thank you for the unexpected unmerited favor you've poured out so freely and graciously.

Amen.

Early Morning with
MINISTER JANEL THOMPSON

9 Much time had been lost, and sailing had already become dangerous because by now it was after the Day of Atonement. So, Paul warned them,

10 "Men, I can see that our voyage is going to be disastrous and bring great loss to ship and cargo, and to our own lives also."

11 But the centurion, instead of listening to what Paul said, followed the advice of the pilot and of the owner of the ship.

Acts 27:9-11 NIV

There were many times in my life I understood a situation to become a *storm,* but those who had charge of me would not listen to my warning or reason to act accordingly. I had the follow their decisions into a *storm*. It is not always our choices that cause suffering in our lives, but it is our belief and relationship with Jesus that sustains us.

Sometimes, God will send you into a storm, so He can have a reason to save others. Saving you in your act of obedience can allow the stage to be set for those around you to know Jesus and His saving grace.

My faith in that storm helped others see Jesus as Healer.

Prayer

Jesus, help me be strong in my faith. Forgive me when I falter.

Amen.

IT'S ME OH LORD

Early Morning with

PASTOR GENAE KULAH

Therefore, let us approach the throne of grace with boldness, so that we may receive mercy and find grace to help us at the proper time.

Hebrews 4:16

When times are going well, we generally do not have a hard time praying to God. We rush to give God praise worship and adoration, because during those times we can see God moving in our lives and feel His presence daily. But what about those times when we cannot feel His presence and our prayers appear to be hitting the ceiling and falling back down. We have too much to do and not enough time to do it. The children are acting out. The car breaks down. We did something that we should not have done. Not to mention that we do not have time to study the bible or have a quiet time, because someone always wants or needs something. We are plain overwhelmed, which causes us to pull back from people, church, and even God. Our emotions tell us that God is not hearing us although the bible says in Psalms 34:15 "The eyes of the LORD are on the righteous, and His ears are open to their cry for help." So, what are we to do?

We are to Walk-UP BOLDLY to the throne of grace in prayer to……

Obtain mercy- kindness or forgiveness shown especially to somebody a person has power over. If we confess our sins, He is faithful and righteous to forgive us our sins and to cleanse us from all unrighteousness I John 1:9

Obtain grace- the free and unmerited favor of God- The LORD is gracious and merciful; Slow to anger and great in lovingkindness Psalm 145:8

Obtain help- God is our refuge and strength, a helper who is always found in times of trouble. Psalm 46:1

Obtain love- But God proves His own love for us in that while we were still sinners, Christ died for us! Romans 5:8

God is concerned about us not just as believers but as His children. He knows the number of every hair on our heads and according to Psalms 56:8 He keeps track of all our sorrows. He has collected all our tears in His bottle. He has recorded each one in His book.

Prayer

Jesus, thank you for loving me so much that You paid the price for me to be able to come directly to You without a middleman. When my heart is overwhelmed, I can run to you, because you are waiting with open arms.

Amen.

IT'S ME OH LORD

Early Morning with

DR. ONIKA SHIRLEY

And without faith it is impossible to please God.

Hebrews 11:6

Now Faith is the substance of things hoped for,

the evidence of things not seen.

Hebrews 11:1

The more I think about faith the more I know I have to walk by faith and not by sight.

I don't just hope for things to happen in my life, but I believe by faith that things will happen in my life. I started to grab a hold of the unseen realm of hope and brought it into the images of my reality. I begin to see the vison of my hope in my life and then things started to happen. Hebrews 11:1 says "Now faith is..." If your faith is not now, then it's not the substance to water your hope for your today's reality. When you grasp the concept of faith, you have unlocked the door to receive whatever it is you are desiring to happen from God. God is so faithful to His word and I have tried him for myself. You receive from God only by faith. Faith will tell you with boldness, "It's yours. I have it now." You should believe that you have whatever it is you are asking God for before you ever actually see it. Circumstances can make you question your life, but you don't have to question God's word because it changes not. If you want to please God, you must trust Him and believe in God and His word by faith.

Prayer

Heavenly Father I thank you for giving me a measure of faith. God, I know that it is impossible to please you without it. God you have given me what I needed to please you and it leaves me without an excuse as to why I don't have it. Thank you, God. I will walk by faith the rest of my life.

Amen.

Early Morning with
STEVII A. MILLS

But the one who does not know and does things deserving punishment will be beaten with few blows. From everyone who has been given much, much will be demanded; and from the one who has been entrusted with much, much more will be asked.

Luke 12:48

I stand Luke 12:48 - I live my life based on the foundations of this scripture. You may be like me - high achieving, goal setting, Christ-loving entrepreneur, whose business is actually their ministry. God has allowed you and I to be, do and have so much that we know that we must give back. That is why our businesses look different and that's why we stay blessed because we know that we have to sow into great ground. God's people are great ground. This is why we have a difficult time actually putting a price on our services and products because we know that without Him there is no us.

Being someone who lives by this scripture has allowed me to become not only a better person but grow a better business. It allows me to over deliver to people and it allows me to always make sure that the foundation of my business is integrity and credibility. My business and your business do not have the luxury to be anything less than excellent. Excellence is required.

Prayer

Father God in the name of Jesus, never let me forget that the occupation is also my vocation – my life and business are my ministry. All that I do, I do unto you. **Amen.**

Early Morning with

CHRISTINA WILSON

Look at the nations and watch- and be utterly amazed. For I am going to do something in your days that you would not believe, even if you were told"

Habakkuk 1:5

I will give you every place you set your foot, as I promised Moses.

Joshua 1:3

Ask me, and I will make the nations your inheritance, the ends of the earth your possession.

Psalms 2:8

Sometimes, oftentimes it's hard to focus on the promise of God put on your heart when it seems like everything is going opposite of that. When you start to feel as if God has forgotten his end of the deal, like your promise has been forgotten it's so easy to find yourself in fits of worry and anxiety. I speak from experience that slowly falling out of faith as things begin to elevate and the world around you become unfamiliar territory. When the safety net falls from underneath you and you're forced to trust in Him for all you need, remember that He promises to give you the desire of your heart. He put the promise on your heart because He plans to provide you with everything, He makes you dream of. Remember that if God makes sure the ravens in the trees have all they need, how much more will he provide for you?! In all things, through all seasons worship the Lord our God in spirit and in truth and remember that His promises will always come to pass. Thank him for it in advance. Keep a praise on your lips and a thanks in your heart for the dreams he has given you and the dreams He will make a reality for YOU!

Early Morning with
DR. ONIKA SHIRLEY

The Lord is my strength and my song, and he has become my salvation.

Exodus 15:2

Often times when we think of the word strength, we seldom think in terms associated with power lifting or muscle building. As women were much more likely to think in terms of emotional stability or resilience. We think in terms of our ability to persevere after spending countless hours caring for our children and other love ones. Women has had to dry countless tears- both from their families and a lot of their own. When others see all that one has to go through they consider them to be a "tower of strength" Women that knows the Lord is their strength they are able to encourage others even when they are going through and so many find them to be their rock. Every living being has its share of troubles, turmoil, and tragedy. We write our plans, but life keeps on happening despite of what we have written down on the paper. We may try to get by on will power or on a positive attitude. We may look to the good deeds, the gifts and talents, or the wisdom of other people to pull us through. These approaches are feeble and over time shows to be of little help. We must learn to lean on the Jesus. Things are going to happen but keep the whole truth in mind. Remember our Savior's strength and his promises to see us through.

Prayer

Lord Jesus, place a song of praise in my heart and on my lips today as I learn to lean on you for strength. Lord I have come to the realization that I can't do life without you and honestly, I don't want to.

Amen.

IT'S ME OH LORD

Early Morning with

PASTOR DENISE ELBERT

A time to weep, and a time to laugh;

a time to mourn, and a time to dance;

Ecclesiastes 3:4 (ESV)

A joyful heart is good medicine...

Proverbs 17:22 (ESV)

I am an employee wellness specialist with a vast position description that ranges from suicide ideation to general morale boosting! Many people know me as the person who brings the 'happy' to their work centers. When you are constantly bombarded with stories of despair and depression along with throwing out a lifeline here and there, toxicity is a workplace hazard! This kind of work required a dose of humor is a part of my daily detox regimen! I've always love to laugh, as a child, I watched lots of comedy shows on TV, some of my favs are "I Love Lucy", and "Golden Girls". After a long workday my 'all-time' detox show was "Duck Dynasty" (when it was on and before the controversy). "Duck Dynasty" allowed me to laugh and then pray at the end of each episode, a wonderful combination!

The word "laugh" (with variations) appears 44 times in English Standard Version of the Holy Bible. Several of the verses use the word to mean to scoff or to mock, not merriment! In the aforementioned verse, "laugh" means unspeakable joy and full of glory! We know that the Lord created us to have a joyful heart; it can come from deep belly laughs. The writer of both verses, King

Solomon, only asked for wisdom and the Lord gave him so much more. His wisdom has been recorded for us to live by and he knew God had created us with healing within. Laughter is good medicine! According to the Mayo clinic, laughter enhances your intake of oxygen-rich air. That means your heart, lungs and muscles are all stimulated. Laughter also cools down your stress response and it can increase then decrease your heart rate and blood pressure, giving you a good relaxed feeling. When I laugh, tension leaves my body, which is another benefit stated by the scientists. Let us take the time to lighten the load of this life with a little humor.

Laughter does the body good!

Prayer

Dear Lord, let the challenges of this life fall away in our laughter.

Amen.

Early Morning with

PASTOR GENAE KULAH

Have nothing to do with irreverent, silly myths. Rather train yourself for godliness;

1 Timothy 4:7

We all have on one or more occasion complained that there are not enough hours in the day to complete everything we must do. And in all honesty, it is absolutely correct. We are all over the place, because we continue to add more and more stuff to our plate then wonder where the time has gone. We set goals only to see them not come to pass because we have allowed another goal to take the place of the first goal. We get caught up in the latest gossip (I mean prayer request) that we do not have time to study the word of God.

We pray and cry pray and cry again for God to help us. When in fact we do not need Him to help us, but we need to take responsibility for our own lives and decide to discipline ourselves. We willingly do what we want to do, so we are where we are because of our choices. We spend too much time on things that are not assisting us in reaching our goal or more importantly the godly purposes that we were designed to fulfill. To fulfill those purposes, we must get on the discipline train to godliness.

We do that by:

- Prioritizing- Keep things in order. God, Family, Church, Work. Balance is our Goal

- Praying- Ask God to show you what He wants you to do. Not all needs are yours to meet.

- Praising- In all things give thanks. It is amazing how things bother us less when we have a grateful attitude.

- Studying- Not just for teaching but for living. You cannot give what you have not first received.

- Worshiping- We must come to God wanting just Him. Not asking for anything but His heart.

When we discipline ourselves to live godly, we reflect the glory of the Lord in everything we do and point a lost world to the only one who can save, the Lord Jesus Christ. We will never be the same.

Prayer

Lord help me to prioritize my life, so that in all things I will bring you glory.

Amen

Early Morning with
DR. ONIKA SHIRLEY

You are altogether beautiful, my love;

there is no flaw in you.

Song of Solomon 4:7

Oh, Precious child of God, adopted by God amazing grace, you possess something so lovely. When you belong to the royal your possession is more valuable than silver and gold. You got Jesus. Jesus` presence graces our lives. He is beautiful, faithful, precious, lovely, and flawless. The very moment he enters our hearts, his beauty begins to influence our lives. At this very moment, child of God you're being transformed, renovated, renewed, and made over. Transformation never happens overnight and sometimes we may feel that it is not happening at all. But as we continue to read the word of God, trust in God, and keep confessing our sins, the man that died for us on Calvary's cross is so faithful to keep on forgiving us. God has promised this to us. But his promise doesn't not end there! "He is also faithful to cleanse us from all unrighteousness" (1 John 1:9). Your renewed heart is Christ's home and you are different as a result. Day by day, Jesus is rearranging your priorities, emptying the stuff you have hidden behind closed doors, and beautifying the inside of you. Day by day, you are becoming more peaceful, less self-centered, more compassionate, more loving, less fearful of the what ifs, and more forgiving. Day by Day, Jesus' presence is changing you.

Prayer

Lord Jesus, you are great. You are beautiful, faithful, precious, and flawless. I want to be just like you. Lord, continue to work on me day by day where the change on the inside will be seen on the outside as I be a witness for you. Lord, I know my transformation will not be over night. I am patiently waiting for you to work on me, mold me, make me, and use me for your glory.

Amen

Early Morning with

DR. ONIKA SHIRLEY

The Lord waits to be gracious to you, and therefore he exalts himself to show mercy to you.

Isaiah 30.18

The Lord will make you personally feel like you are the center of attention in the mist of crowd and still be no respecter of person. He will open doors for you, protect you, serve you, and make things more convenient for you. When you have someone willing to do so much for you the last place you want to place him is on the back burner. You want to be concerned about what he thinks, and you want to be willing to do what he has commanded. You should make sure that your relationship with our Savior is priority and that it stays at the top of your list every day. The Almighty could insist on a change and the way we think but what fun is that to force someone to love you. He could force his people to cringe in fear and shame. He could even pitch us into unconsciousness instead he graciously waits. He urges us, through his prophets, to repent of our sins and to recalibrate our priorities. Although sin breaks the heart of God, he will not force us to be obedient. Even when he brings his almighty power to bear, he does that only so that he can show mercy, bring his amazing grace and forgiveness to a repentant people. Today God is still waiting. Our loving Lord never trespasses, never forces his love, his relationship, nor his gifts. His endeavor is always to help up and not hurt us. The finished work of Christ on the Cross proves it. God is always a gentleman and He does what is best for us even when we don't know or understand what that is.

Prayer

Lord, you are amazing, and your grace is gentle. Thank you, Father.

Amen

Early Morning with
PASTOR DENISE ELBERT

"...for the joy of the Lord is your strength" Nehemiah 8:10 (MEV)

When I answered my call to ministry and signed all my correspondence, "Joyfully in Jesus". I thought it was catchy. I knew it was a true reflection of who I was in Christ! In my 20's I learned that nothing could steal my joy...not a lack of funds, lack of friends, or a lack of virtues (I was still maturing). Anyone watching me could see that I had an inner joy that kept me going!

In Nehemiah 8:10, as Ezra read the law, the people stood for hours in reverence of God's Word, they realized they sinned and began to weep. Their sorrow is like ours today, trying times that push us to do things we wouldn't normally do, like hoard food and toilet tissue or not show compassion to the suffering. Our selfish sinful ways can leave us weary and wondering where our strength is! But God...Ezra reminds us, as he did in his day, that the Joy of the Lord is my strength. To understand this, I recall something I heard in church, "This joy I have, the world didn't give it to me...! That's right this is not mere human joy, this is joy that comes from our God!

My four steps to this joy are simple:

1. Go deeper in the Word; **#readyourbible** and study it!

2. See God in everything! One morning I pumped gasoline in my car and the end dollar amount matched the numbers in my birthday, my

response…Hello to you too, God! He is everywhere and in everything, look for Him.

3. Pray in all things. Talk to God first!

4. Act now, you are ready, you are strong!

Early Morning with
DR. ONIKA SHIRLEY

He said to me, "My grace is sufficient for you, for my power is made perfect in weakness." Therefore I will boast all the more gladly of my weaknesses, so that the power of Christ may rest upon me.

2 Corinthians 12:9

I have enough is a phrase we don't hear too often. We don't hear many children say they have enough toys. We don't hear coaches say we have enough victories. We don't hear adults say I have enough money. We don't hear many women say they've went to enough shoe sales. We just never hardly hear "Enough." The Lord calmed Paul's fearful heart with the simple words "My grace is enough" God told his apostle that his grace was all he needed. Paul thought he needed more and how often do we think we need more of something. The Apostle Paul thought he needed deliverance from a specific problem that bothered him. The man of God saw this problem as a barrier, as an obstacle, and a hindrance to his ministry. No, God said my grace is sufficient. Paul more than likely did not quite understand, but in the end, he submitted to the wisdom of the Lord. He gladly accepted his weaknesses because God's grace was enough and completely enough and for that Paul was thankful. You too will encounter challenges in your life it's not a matter of if but when we are not exempt. But for you and me, God's grace is always enough. It's enough to keep us pressing and enough to see us through.

Prayer

Lord Jesus, your amazing grace is truly enough for us. When we're tempted to demand or even think more, please show us your sufficient grace supply. Knowing that your grace is enough makes our hearts grateful. Thankful hearts are loving and giving hearts. God your grace makes a great difference.

Amen.

Creating my own devotions has been on the most powerful tools in my Christina walk. The LORD has always met me at the point on my need based on my ability to formulate the words to ASK, SEEK and KNOCK!

Read: Matthew 7:7-12

Write your own devotions on the pages provided; don't stop here, grab a journal or a notebook and keep on creating.

IT'S ME OH LORD

Early Morning with ME

Early Morning with ME

IT'S ME OH LORD

Early Morning with ME

IT'S ME OH LORD

Early Morning with ME

Early Morning with ME

Meet your Early Morning devotion sisters.

ABOUT MARILYN E PORTER

Marilyn Elizabeth Porter, widely known among friends and colleagues as "M.E." is a woman after God's own heart with a passion for people and purpose - and just a tad bid of education and business knowledge. A native Jersey Girl, she has lived in various locations throughout the U.S. and Europe - she currently resides Metro Atlanta.

Marilyn is a woman of *integrity* and *vision* and believes God for every single step she takes in her life, business, and ministry. As a mother, minister, and mogul in the making, she believes in ensuring that God gets the glory in all of decisions. Although she is often plagued with procrastination, she believes in moving in excellence, especially concerning ministry.

Marilyn holds a BS in Psychology, MS in Management and Leadership Development and in 2016 was awarded an Honorary Doctorate in Ministry Development. She believes in education but depends on her God - given wisdom as her primary source of success.

She is the Founder and Overseer of The Pink Pulpit International Convention of Women in Ministry.

www.marilyneporter.com

www.facebook.com/marilynporter

www.ppicwomen.com

Ministry prayer line: 706-528-0625

ABOUT GENAE KULAH

Pastor Genae Kulah is a woman after God's own heart. She is the founder and fearless leader of The Word 4 Her Ministries – where is teaches and trains women in the way of The Gospel of Jesus Christ. She is a life coach, author and serves as the Prophetic Voice and the Executive Pastor of The PPIC. Pastor Genae resides on Compton, CA with her sons and a host of fur babies.

https://www.facebook.com/theword4her/

ABOUT DENISE ELBERT

Pastor Denise Elbert is an encourager to all., in all aspects of her life – encouragement is her ministry. She is the Lead Pastor of The PPIC and plays a role is supporting bot the Overseer and the Executive Pastor. Pastor D is dedicated Greek Sister of Delta Sigma Theta, Inc. and is an award-winning Toastmaster. She is the mother of 2 adult children and the Go-Go to 2 beautiful granddaughters and a 1 handsome grandson.

ABOUT ONIKA SHIRLEY

Dr. Onika L. Shirley, the founder and CEO of Action Speaks Volume, Inc. is a Child of God, Global Confidence and Procrastination Coach and Motivational Speaker. She is a Christian Counselor, founder of ASV's Orphanage Home in India, Sewing Center in Pakistan, Empowering Eight Inner Circle and was blessed and grateful to have a coaching client all the way in Namibia, Africa. She is impacting the lives of many around the world.

https://actionspeaksvolum.com
www.facebook.com/actionspeaksvolume
www.facebook.com/onikashirley
www.twitter.com/actionspeaksvo2
www.instagram.com/actionspeaksvolume

Onika's Dedication

I dedicate this book To God Almighty my creator, my children, and to my precious granddaughter Aubrey A. Franklin. Father God, I love you.

ABOUT CASSANDRA ELLIOTT

Pastor Cassandra Elliott is a walking example of the Five-Fold Ministry. A native of New York City, and the Wife of Mr. Bryant Elliott, Pastor Elliott found her ministry beginnings in the world of music. Currently serving as a Pastor of Worship her gift has carried her internationally. Pastor Elliott is known for her passion for ministry even in places of unexpected pain and trial. She is a survivor of Kidney Disease and Breast Cancer and has used both of these testimonies as a vehicle to encourage others through the preached, taught, and imparting Word of God and worship.

www.cassandraelliottministries.com
www.Facebook.com/PCCassandraElliott
www.Instragram.com/Iamcassandraelliott

IT'S ME OH LORD

https://www.linkedin.com/in/casandra-elliott-96b45723

ABOUT JANEL THOMPSON

Minister Janel Thompson has one goal, sharing the love, hope and peace of the Gospel of Christ Jesus. She is the wife of Matthew and mother to her daughters, Taliyah and Zaneta. Minister Thompson has faced many challenges as a Sickle Cell Warrior but with the power of God she lives a blessed and abundant life. Janel accepted her call to ministry at the age of 15 and has since served under several ministries, including liturgical dance, children's ministry and as a Global Ambassador for Pink Pulpit. She was licensed in November of 2017 by Dr. Marilyn E. Porter founder of the Pink Pulpit. Minister

Thompson's future plans include finishing her theology degree and becoming an ordained Pastor.

"I love the Lord because He has made me whole, Colossians **2:10**".

ABOUT STEVII MILLS

Stevii Aisha Mills embraces a culture where fun is not just a niche, it is a necessity! Stevii is a proud graduate of North Carolina A&T State University, where Aggie Pride reigns. Her formal education consists of a BA in Public Relations and a MS in Human Resources, however Stevii's real life experiences have made her well-known social media influencer and gained her the title "The Chief It Factor Cultivator"! A woman unashamed to incorporate tons of fun into her life and business, while declaring, "I love my life!", has made Stevii a highly sought out speaker.

My website is www.howtomakeittothenews.com

My email is stevii@stevii.com

ABOUT TIESHA FRONTIS

Tiesha C. Frontis, BS, CCTA is a serial momprenuer, International Best-Selling author, philanthropist, mentor, radio, television, and conference host, as well as a mental health activist. She is a visionary, and the founder of Know Your-Self Worth International Ministries, Inc. (KYSW). She holds a Bachelor of Science in Chemistry and Bachelor of Science in Biology from North Carolina Central University. She is a leader in the community and serves as the District Director for ACHI Women Supporting Women Association. Tiesha also owns and operates the following businesses: 1st Choice Clinical Solutions, NonPro Management, HerGems Boutique, The Chic Lips and MiBell Beauty Bar.

www.knowyourselfworth.org

www.1stchoiceclinicalsolutions.com

www.nonpromgt.com

www.hergemsboutique.com

www.thechiclips.com

www.bit.ly/mibellbeautybar.com

ABOUT JUANITA E GAYNOR

Juanita Estelle Gaynor is a Philadelphia native who relocated to Atlanta, GA in 2008; She holds an Associate degree in Business Administration from Eastern Nazarene College and an Associate degree in Accounting from Atlanta Technical College. She is a long-time entrepreneur and currently has 3companies (EABJ Consulting, Elite Financial Mgmt., and Restored 2 Life), Host and Producer of *Moving Past You Radio Show* and *Viola's Daughter: A*

Survivor's Story. My goal is to always be the light that God has purposed me to be.

ABOUT CHRISTINA WILSON

Christina Wilson is a 23-year-old actress from the small town of Temple Georgia by way of Fredericksburg Maryland. She has been in the entertainment industry for eight years focusing on acting, writing, directing, and producing. She owns her own production company Twelve Two Productions and spends her time teaching youth life skills through art. "I want to show people that God is in the entertainment industry just as much as the church house" Christina is also the 2nd child of Marilyn Porter's trio of beautiful daughters.

www.Instagram.com/_TinaNotTurner

Youtube - Tina Not Turner / TwelveTwoProductions

OTHER TITLES
AVAILABLE ON AMAZON

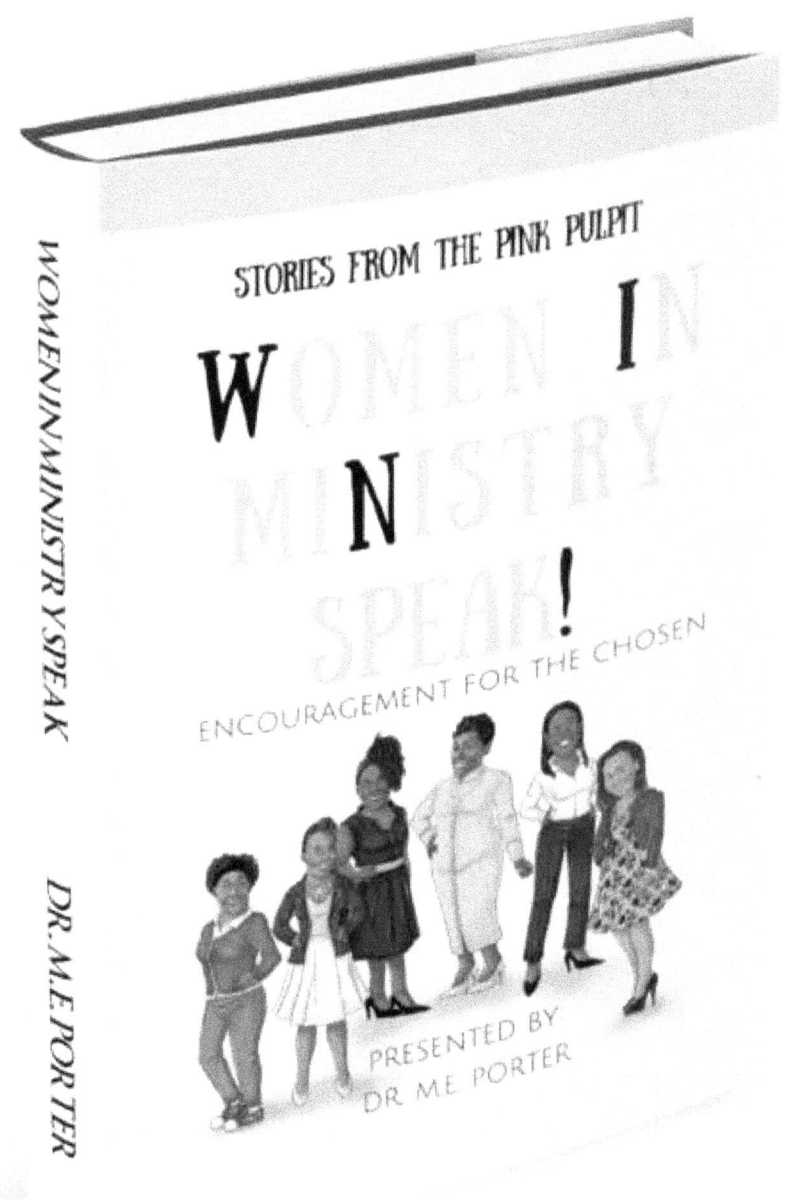

HERSTORY

Reveals His Glory

AND THEY OVERCAME BY THE BLOOD OF THE LAMB AND THE POWER OF THEIR STORIES

DR ME PORTER
COLLABORATION PROJECT

Herstory Reveals His Glory — M.E. Porter

www.ingramcontent.com/pod-product-compliance
Lightning Source LLC
Chambersburg PA
CBHW080448110426
42743CB00016B/3313